Saint Isidora

The Monastery Sponge

Written by
Kh. Cindy Anne Hogg

Illustrated by
Kh. Emily Harju

Copyright © 2023 Exaltation Press

Author: Kh. Cindy Anne Hogg
Illustrator: Kh. Emily Harju

"St. Isidora - The Monastery Sponge"
   This book tells the story of St. Isidora of Tabenna, one of the first saints to be called a "fool for Christ." In a way appropriate for children, it helps them understand this important and unique way in which some of the saints have lived out their life in Christ by deliberately not seeking the honor and respect of anyone except God Himself.

All rights reserved. This book or any portion thereof may not be reproduced or used in any manner whatsoever without the express written permission of the publisher except for the use of brief quotations in a book review.

ISBN: 978-1-950067-16-9 (Paperback)

First printing edition 2023

Exaltation Press
Grand Rapids, MI

www.ExaltationPress.com

For bulk orders, please contact editor@exaltationpress.com.

St. Isidora – The Monastery Sponge

Do you know what a sponge is? Perhaps you have seen one in your kitchen, or used one to soak up spills or wash dishes. Some people use a large sponge to wash their car.

Sponges are absorbent when they are dry. That means they soak things, like water, up into themselves. When they are wet, they can be used to scrub things that are dirty. Wet or dry, that's what sponges are used for: to clean things up.

But how can a person be a sponge?

The saint I am going to tell you about today was called "the monastery sponge" by the other nuns she lived with. Let me tell you, dear reader, that was not a nickname given in love. Oh, no, it was meant as an insult to make her feel bad.

But, as always, God has the last word!

Before she was a saint, Isidora was a young girl living in Egypt. Do you know where Egypt is? Egypt is a large country in the northeastern corner of the African continent. Try to find it sometime on a map or globe.

A monastic is a man or woman who doesn't marry and who devotes his or her life completely to God. Christian monasticism began in the Egyptian deserts. Monastics went into the desert to get away from all the distractions of the world and to follow the examples of Old Testament saints like Elijah and Moses. (You may remember that Elijah and Moses appeared with Christ on the Mount of Transfiguration.) John the Baptist lived in the desert for much of his life. Even Jesus Christ retreated to the desert when he was tempted for 40 days. What good examples the monastics were following!

Early monastics used to live alone in the desert. In the 4th century, St. Pachomius formed the first community of monastics who lived together to serve and support each other. His monastery was for men and was located in Tabenna. Later, his sister Maria founded a nearby monastery for women. It was here that Isidora took herself to serve God as a monastic.

We do not know when Isidora was born or anything about her family or life before she came to the Tabenna monastery – or even exactly when she came to the monastery. But our story concerns what happened to Isidora after she came to the monastery.

Things happened to Isidora because she was a "sponge." Instead of absorbing water as we know it, Isidora absorbed the Living Water. Do you know who the Living Water is? That's right, it's Jesus Christ!

How did she absorb Jesus Christ? First of all, by being baptized, which is where every Christian becomes joined to Christ. Secondly, she absorbed Him by studying all the words that He spoke to His disciples and all the words of sacred scripture. She did not just study them with her mind but truly took them into her heart and soul, striving to fully live by them every day.

Isidora was struck by St. Paul's words in 1 Cor. 3:18: "Whosoever of you believes that he is wise by the measure of this world, may he become a fool, so as to become truly wise." Isidora determined she would become a "fool for Christ." Over the years, other Christians have become "fools for Christ," but Isidora was one of the very first.

More than 400 women lived at the monastery in Tabenna, and Isidora decided she would serve Christ and her sisters by doing all the lowliest jobs there. She worked mostly in the kitchen, where she wore a dishrag on her head instead of a head covering like the other nuns. The sisters of the monastery thought she was crazy. They made fun of her and would not let her eat with the rest of them.

Isidora didn't mind. She wanted to be alone so she could pray and praise God without interruptions. She ate just the crumbs the other sisters left behind and drank the dishwater left after washing the dishes. She never got angry with anyone or spoke an unkind word, even when others were mean to her. She never complained or grumbled about her tasks, always trusting God in everything.

Now if you think that Isidora was a "monastery sponge" because she absorbed the spiritual life of the monastery and because she did all the menial cleaning jobs there, you would be right - but not completely right. God used her in an even more important way to "clean up" the monastery.

This is how it happened.

A wise and well-respected hermit lived in the desert during this time. His name was St. Piteroum. One day when he was praying, an angel appeared to him and said, "Why are you proud of being a hermit who says so many prayers? When you say your prayers, your mind flits all about. But at the monastery in Tabenna, there is a woman who is much more pious than you, for her prayers are focused and genuine. Go there and you will see her wearing a crown upon her head."

To understand the angel's words, you have to know what it means to "flit about." Have you ever watched little birds? They often "flit about" by jumping or hopping here and there in a seemingly haphazard way.

Now think about your prayers. When you are praying, does your mind ever jump to thinking about playing with your friends or what you're about to eat?

It is the same for many of us. The angel praised Isidora because she did not let other thoughts distract her from her prayers. She did not care what others thought of her. She only cared about what God thought of her.

St. Piteroum received a blessing to travel to the Tabenna monastery. There he asked to meet the sisters. After meeting all 400 of them, he felt disappointed. "Are there no other sisters who reside here?" he asked.

"Well, there is one more," the sisters told him, "but you would not want to meet her. She is crazy!"

Truthfully, St. Isidora did not want to meet St. Piteroum either. She did not want her prayers to be interrupted, and she didn't want to be singled out for attention. Nonetheless, the sisters brought Isidora to meet the saint. When they did, she bowed down before him but he fell down before her and asked her blessing, exclaiming, "This is the one! See the crown of glory upon her head!"

A crown? But Isidora only had a dishrag on her head!

Do you remember the crown of thorns they placed upon the head of Jesus before they crucified him? That was not a crown as we usually think of one either. But that is because we are looking at these "crowns" with human eyes, and not the way God sees them – as signs of true greatness in the most important ways.

And so, the sisters had their spiritual eyes opened, and they immediately felt very ashamed. They began to confess to St. Piteroum.

"We have been so mean to Isidora! We have called her names and made fun of her behind her back!" One nun confessed that she had even hit Isidora and another confessed that she had dumped food on her! The sisters begged St. Piteroum to forgive them and of course, they asked Isidora to forgive them also - which she did. After that, they changed their ways and all treated Isidora much better.

Do you see how God used this "monastery sponge" to clean up the sinful thoughts and actions of others?

Perhaps this story reminds you a little bit of Cinderella. As you recall, Cinderella had to do all the menial tasks and cleaning around the house and people were mean to her. In spite of this, Cinderella never complained and was kind to those who treated her badly. When the prince's soldiers brought the glass slipper around to all the houses and no foot was found to fit it, they asked, "Is there not some other girl to try it on?" Cinderella's sisters said, "There is one more, but you will not want dirty old Cinderella to try it on."

Of course, we all know how the Cinderella story ends!

But what of Isidora? Isidora did not like all the attention she was now receiving at the monastery. It embarrassed her and she could no longer pray as she once had. God had finished using her to teach a lesson to others, so kind, pious, humble Isidora left the monastery to live alone in peace and piety. She lived such a quiet and obscure life that no one knows for sure when she died. We believe it was around the year 365 AD.

Dear reader, is it wrong to care about what others think about us? Of course not. We want our parents to be proud of us and our friends to think well of us. But so very often we begin to care too much about what others think of us. It's so easy to forget that the most important thing is what God thinks of us.

Like Cinderella, Isidora lived happily ever after. But not with the earthly riches of a prince and castle – things which are rarely real and which will one day pass away as they are only temporary. Isidora's treasures are the ones that last forever, the ones that can never be taken away. Isidora is part of a kingdom that will last "forever and ever, unto ages of ages. Amen." And while Cinderella is just a made-up fairy tale, St. Isidora's story is a true one about a real girl who lived and loved her Lord.

When the Lord chastened Saint Piteroum for 'traveling in the cities' mentally while living as a solitary, he was instructed to seek you, O Isidora, fool for Christ. The nuns, seeing only foolishness, did not discern your unceasing prayer to Christ God whom you loved with your heart, soul, mind, and strength. Focusing on the rags upon your head, they missed your resplendent crown of love!

St. Isidora's feast days are May 1 & 10. St. Isidora, pray for us!

Troparion of St. Isidora, the Fool of Tabenna:
In thee, O mother, that which was created according to the image of God was manifestly saved; For, taking up thy cross, thou didst follow after Christ; and, praying, thou didst learn to disdain the flesh, for it passeth away, but to care for thy soul as a thing immortal. Wherefore, with the angels thy spirit doth rejoice, O venerable Isidora.

Kontakion of the venerable one:
Having acquired the mind of Christ, O divinely wise one, Thou didst reject the wisdom of this world; Showing the appearance of foolishness to men, But worshiping God with understanding; Meditating on His wisdom every hour, filled with the Holy Spirit. Wherefore, we all cry out: Rejoice, O Isidora, thou boast of Tabenna!

www.ingramcontent.com/pod-product-compliance
Lightning Source LLC
Chambersburg PA
CBHW051809100526
44592CB00016B/2634